Humor Me

Humor Me

Claudia Gary-Annis

David Robert Books

Published by David Robert Books
P.O. Box 541106
Cincinnati, OH 45254-1106

Typeset in Aldine by WordTech Communications LLC, Cincinnati, OH

ISBN: 1932339884
LCCN: 2004098665

Poetry Editor: Kevin Walzer
Business Editor: Lori Jareo

Visit us on the web at www.davidrobertbooks.com

Acknowledgments

Grateful acknowledgment is made to the editors of literary journals in which most of these poems first appeared, sometimes in earlier versions:

Black Buzzard Review: "Lost Satellite"

Edge City Review: "Disclaimer to Accompany 'Love' Stamp," "Postal Riposte," "Judicious Self-Gratification," "Millennium WWWitches' Brew," "Wedding Poem," "Dormancy," "Indecision," "The Conjugal Bookcase," "Voice of the Cicadas," "Garden Statues," "Midlife Interrogation," "A Fault," "Ripples in the Fabric," "To One Who Listens," "Audit," "The Old Year," "Teletype Circa 1976," "Lactose Intolerance"

The Formalist: "The Topiarist," "Schadenfreud(e)," "The Test," "Trading Up," "Song of the Diarist's Wife," "Angel Encounter"

Light: "News of a Bull Market," "Pleasures Disproven," "A Birthday Reply," "Authority," "A Falling-Out," "Preparing for a Visit," "Call Waiting," "So sorry, Shall I Call Back Later?"

The Lyric: "In Fog," "After-Image"

Medicinal Purposes: "Song of the Off-Duty Psychiatrist," "What I Have Missed," "Phonograph," "The Love Seat," "Colorization," "Etude"

Neovictorian/Cochlea: "Daphne's Regrets," "Encounter II," "The Perfect Word"

Northern Virginia Review: "Findings"

Orbis (U.K.): "Interdisciplinary Ode"

Pivot: "Labyrinth"

Poetry Digest: "The Snow Woman," "The Snowsuit Photograph"

Reston Review: "Mother's Day 1990," "A Gift," "Along the Potomac," "To the Evening Sky"

Sparrow: "Fame's Aftertaste," "Interdisciplinary Ode," "The Quill," "Vitreous Floater," "The New Formalossus," "The Cricket"

Some of the poems have also been reprinted in the following places:

ART Ideas: "Cherry Blossom Time".

Expansive Poetry & Music Online: various poems

Fairfax Journal/Express: "To One Who Listens"

The Hypertexts: various poems

Journal of the American Association of Massage Therapists: "Interdisciplinary Ode"

Kiss and Part (ed. Gail White; Doggerel Daze, 2005): "Pleasures Disproven"

Loudoun Art: "Midlife Interrogation"

Public Pamphlet: "To the Evening Sky," "Cherry Blossom Time"

Reston Connection: "Voice of the Cicadas"

The 80ᵗʰ Anniversary Anthology of the Poetry Society of Virginia: "Song of the Diarist's Wife," "Teletype Circa 1976," "Midlife Interrogation," "Preparing for a Visit," "Pleasures Disproven," "Colorization," "Trading Up"

Winchester Star: "Call Waiting"

Words and Pictures Online: various poems

To locate internet publications, see links on the author's Web site at http://claudiagary.home.att.net

for Richard Moore

"It may be that one's attitude toward meter will often come down to one's attitude to poetry's monuments—to Milton, say, or Shakespeare. If you...see them as poets who fashioned still relevant masterpieces...then you will be inclined to study them in hope of gaining some understanding of their secrets; you will see them and their age as possible repositories of a lost wisdom, detectable even in the music of their verse."—Richard Moore, *The Rule that Liberates*

Contents

I. *The Conjugal Bookcase*

Teletype, circa 1976

No other medium could grant our wish
to dance together on a gleaming floor
of coated newsprint, clasping one another's
next letter in a frantic reach of words.

No telephone could replicate the warm
click-clicking of our heels disguised as keys,
stepping across the platen on white paper
and through kilometers of humming wire.

No e-mail could have let me hear you think
between the words, some slow, some at a clip,
some pausing for my answer's foot to fall
or skittering away from other questions:

—*when can we speak again? where can I see you?*—
the hurried editing, the mingled phrases
no longer filling anything but paper.
And then the keys grew cool, the wire quiet.

Labyrinth

No sooner thought than meant—no sooner meaning
than verbiage, though not a word be spoken.
We settle for the twilight intervening
on this cloud-covered stage, this field of broken
alliance, statuary, and intention.

When we awake, a city crowned with spires
surrounds us: a somnambulist's invention
whose maze of pathways mocks at our desires,
whose barriers are poised to resonate
with thoughts we barely utter. Are you sure
that this was what we wanted to create?

Wedding Poem

You can make a fire with a lens of ice
so clear it tunes the sun and does not melt.

You will have a white dress
in which to be yourself and yet a bride.

The Fitting

For Leonore

I.

Try it on, they said.
It wasn't just the bows
and ruffles that annoyed her
but having to discern

through eyelet lace the wide view,
through gathered sleeves the strong grip,
below each frill the clear line
that she was looking for.

But when she saw their eyes,
poor buttonholes devouring
their likenesses in her,
she said: *What if I do?*

What if I try this on,
then leave it here for you
to touch as you remember?

Humor us, they smiled.

II.

Humor me, he said.
It wasn't just to see
the ways her form inhabited
some flimsy cloth, but also

a scene that might unfold:
first the indignant silence
and then the reddened face
gazing at him—he wanted

to see her try *that* on.
But when she caught the mischief
inhabiting his eyes
she said: *What if I do*—

what if I try that on,
all of it, and then soon
it's folded in a corner
entirely forgotten

for days or years until
it settles over me
raggedly, toward the end?

Try it on, he smiled.

The Test

I saw your heart beat silently
within a flat translucent sea,
cradled in waves of sound.

My doctor spun her chair around;
your floating image washed aground
in megahertz and pulse

whose quick but careful intervals
she said would spare the particles
that form your brain and bone.

From pictured sound your age is known,
from child to specimen you've grown:
your cells await their Test.

And if they are not of the best,
what then? What then? Would we invest
long days to nurture pain?

The doctor's quizzing eye is trained
to hint that life may be in vain.
She learned to heal, she vowed to try,
but now her job is hard to classify.

Song of the Expectant Father

She is quiet now,
thoughts folded into baby,
letting pain ripen.

Soothing her, pacing,
calling nurse: these I can do.
Labor I cannot.

Maybe by sunrise
two of us will finally
unfold into three.

Preparing to hold
newborn, I claw worry lines
into a soap bar.

The Quill

Great-Grandpa's masterpiece was just a sketch:
he drew himself while waiting for your words
to tell him there was no more need to stretch
his heavy bones, worn brittle as a bird's;
to tell him he *would* fly through your tableau
etched in the will-have-been, the future-past
he'd outlined there with quill—and thus winged grow
to be the very brightness he had cast
across four generations. He was sly,
convincing me his flickering eyes and ears
had time to watch you crawl, stand, toddle by,
when all he had was patience, honed by years
to master time. Trusting your mind grew tall,
he clenched the brittle pen, then let it fall.

Mother's Day 1990

How fervently she hopes to be discovered,
though tracks have cooled and loosed her quaint perfume;
in your repose you sense that she has hovered
unseen and not quite welcome in your room.
Neither did you invite her in, nor ask
to be invited into her purview,
yet spirited you were, and brought to bask
in her attention. Still she watches you
and tends you, for her steps are often found
unsettled and unsettling in your own
brash footprints, and her voice can still resound
in your entreaties to be left alone.
How deftly she has coaxed you to unearth
what won you her devotion, and your birth.

The Snowsuit Photograph

For Marji

Cousin, here we stand immobilized
on our grandmother's screened-in rowhouse porch
and wonder why she's packaged us this way
in heavy zippered jackets, mittens, hoods,
when we would love snowflakes to settle secretly
into our curls and brush our fingertips.
Boots tugging woolen pants, we'll walk down brick steps
into the frosted sheet cake of her garden,
stomping to crack the icing, but at six and three
too ladylike to throw it at each other.
We'll probably build a slushy gentleman
whose image ends up in a cardboard box,
unlike this favorite picture of benign
childhood paralysis. We can't wait to change.

You raise your daughter in the tropics now.
Mine balances her brother in a sled—
together they roar down the hill once more
soaked to the freezing skin, invincible.

Dormancy

They do look beautiful sleeping.
Soon they will own the day
and spend their own somnambulance,
free to pursue our likeness:

slopes of our faces grown younger,
continuous rooms of our voices,
obliging arcs and contours
for the ones we once consoled.

Tonight they look beautiful sleeping.
From us they will seize the day,
free to pursue somnambulance,
free to misspend our likeness.

Indecision

"...even if [the angels] do not exist, is not the very thought of them an active warrant of their reality as causes? For are not thoughts causes?"
—Frederick Turner, *"Angels from the Time to Come,"*
in Tempest, Flute & Oz

The souls of unborn children? Silly angels,
no wonder you've been in the air tonight
quarreling with each other and with me.
It's all my fault for offering such hope
when only some of you will ever find
substance. This wound that keeps reopening
and claiming to be love, this awful churning—
it's a whirlpool where you have tried to swim,
now bobbing to the surface, now dragged under.
No wonder you've been quarreling.

You vivid ones, you need no introduction
to the two children sleeping down the hall:
I first saw that boy in a pool of light
like yours, but on a screen. He isn't usually
this quiet. Next door his sister dreams,
she who emerged unstudied, unsurveilled,
perfection never doubted—I suppose
you know them both. They breathe for some of you.

You dimmer angels are the ones who scare me:
Circling lights abuzz like faulty neon
and winking on and off, you try to draw me
down into a discussion I had thought
not a soul could reopen.

In Fog

How dense this dialogue!
      We're hills aloft in fog
            that the lightning fails to quicken.

No tree can bear its fruit,
      no bird can find its mate:
            in the glutinous haze they sicken.

Can you, without a qualm,
      take this incessant calm
            and call it a storm to weather?

Good storms I've clambered through,
      precipitating dew,
            but here in the fog I wither.

There's nothing more to log
      from hills aloft in fog
            that the lightning failed to quicken.

A Gift

Youth's love, no longer young, here is one kiss
that lives solely in telling—not on coals
combusting with a banshee wail as souls
abandon reason. Truth's pleasure exists
translucently: no spark will fly amiss
from ember eyes whose gentleness unfolds
more finely than that breath of emeralds
which was their vernal photosynthesis.

Is it such mystery I've learned to treasure
reason, who thought it cold in years uncouth?
Old love, seeing you now belies love's measure,
unfreezes false economies of youth;
but here's the kiss I owe to you: such pleasure
as can be taken only by the truth.

After-Image

This rose must have been left for me
    decades ago by you,
a gift I never had the sense to see—
      frozen in dew,

methodically sealed away
    within an antique chest
whose key you only forwarded today—
      today be blessed!

And yet the key is fastened to
    a baffling disarray
of blooms in natural and borrowed hue
      to dress this day

in dawns and moons we did not share,
    child-cries we never heard,
laughter (our own) childlike beyond repair,
      reason deferred.

Thawed petals shed a rhapsody
    mere senses can't contain
till temperate breeze whispers your song to me
      with coy refrain:

'I've left a little scar here
*   with rosy shape and hue—*
Examined from a distant year
how much more sweet it may appear
*   than what is true.'*

The Conjugal Bookcase

Our shelves are multilayered now; it couldn't be postponed.
We've scrutinized the theme and plot of every book we owned,
then shifted volumes, purged a few that weren't fitting—those
we never should have opened are the toughest ones to close.

A chapter here is upside-down; to keep an even hand
we've had to choose which portion we prefer to understand.
This system makes a certain kind of sense, though it's complex.
We stash poetry manuals behind the ones on sex.

The photo albums too have undergone repaginations:
whichever eyes peer into ours and threaten palpitations
are slipped behind some other pair that won't go wandering
beyond *The Odyssey* or *How to Fix Most Anything*.

Fair-lettered friends, please understand
     what makes these choices sound.
Please understand it matters less
     whose leaves make our hearts pound
than where, some yet-unnumbered day,
     we're likely to be found.

A Subjunctive Voice

This is a sorrow
you spend on yourself,
chanting to ease its sting.

If only you'd heard
the song before,
if only, if only, you sing.

One mind's music
lost on another
ends with a broken string

that stutters, reaching
for one last word:
If only, if only, you sing.

What I Have Missed

Is it the outermost edge of a candle's flame
where it's safe to touch, in an ancient trick with wind
on the palm of your hand, skirting the waxy frame—

is that what I've missed? Or is it a teardrop's covering,
the salt chemise that won't stay put but opens
to an untold flood, with only a small thought hovering

of you? Or a frail nuance of the words last spoken,
a trail of echoed syllables undone
from the moment of their birth, their cipher broken?

But no, I possess all these. Yet I am kissed
by edges that sear, and melt, and signify
all that the word, the flood, and the flame have missed.

II. *The Love Seat*

Etude

These sounds are only fragments of the dark,
not music, never that;
not even variations on the noon
whose fever they help dissipate.

Here is a careless breeze grown to a gust
and wrestled back; a flapping gate
whose stroke and tap contain and lose the quiet;
the hum of a passing engine.

And yet I seem to coax them into phrases
that start, and end, and echo—
assigning measures to the engine's drone,
giving the gate staccato.

As phrases they can modulate and turn:
The wind becomes a dolorous
sigh that doesn't leave when fever's broken

though music will possess, reject,
possess me and reject me finally
until there is no melody but one.

Phonograph

Remember, dear, when this was the one way
to make a disk sing? Full-size, not compact—
and both the disk and player would obey
only if you possessed your share of tact:
You'd lift the tone arm, puff a bit of air
across its fragile needle to remove
new dust, or use a brush of sable hair
to coax it out. After each vinyl groove
was polished with the softest chamois cloth,
you'd spin a record on its table, place
the needle over it, light as a moth—
you must remember! For the way you trace
the path of every melody *I* store
shows gentleness I've never known before.

A Birthday Reply

(On being wished 100 more years)

Dear love, when you once warned me that you'd wizen
               I'm glad I didn't listen.
Some fifty years from now I'll be all gristle
               and you'll still make me sizzle.
That being said, I hate to call your bluff
               but fifty more's enough.

The Love Seat

On morning's dream-wracked underside
I woke, and there you weren't.
I rubbed away salt crystals left
from last night's weepy torrent
and stumbled to the living room
where, lumpy and abhorrent,

our poor old loveseat cradled
your solitary form
in its chaotic nest, curled up
too peaceful and too warm
to pass as any refugee
from battle, blast, or storm.

No wonder you'd insisted
that after all we keep
this broken-down, ripped-covered,
misshapen, wobbly heap:
you knew that love-crazed quarrels need
the proper place to sleep.

The Refrigerator

Each night you wander silently
in sleep clothes quite becoming
to check once more and see if our
refrigerator's humming.

It's doomed, you say—it's overfilled.
I say life's much too brief
to keep our gripes and worries chilled
and save them for a beef.

When all I have beside me
is your shadow in your stead,
I'll think of ways to warm you
till the phone rings by the bed.

I'll pick up the receiver
from the fingertips of day.
"Is it humming?" you will ask me.
"No, it's quiet now," I'll say.

Song of the Diarist's Wife

There is no need to padlock your poor journal.
I've little to no interest in your cursed
obsession with past lovers—though infernal,
it's no less tedious. Why should I thirst
for some purported juicy inside story
when all of my desire is for you?
If murky rivers wind through purgatory,
why should I clamber for a better view?
And even if you'd mapped out paradise
and found the keys to heighten your immersion
in that celestial realm, I'd say, "That's nice,"
and find my own—not buy into your version.

However, if it's me you write about,
then, hang it all—that *is* worth finding out.

The Chocolate Map

Last night I tried to find you on a chart
confectioners had hidden, darkly framed
over the pleated chambers of a heart-
shaped box, one layer above the sweets it named:

You aren't stuck in Nougat, Chew, or Truffle,
nor clambering through Vermont Pecan Fudge,
nor lost in diplomatic Cherry Cordial
though you too can explode at pinch or nudge.

You're nowhere to be found inside this trove
of blissful states with unspoiled boundaries,
a sticky wilderness where foil and love
are two of many wrappings made to please.

Don't wander off the real map. If you do,
something in here may take my mind off you.

Driving in Tandem

He sped out of her sight numerous times
and left his headlights off in gushing rain.
She wonders how she could have been amused
at flights from visibility.

He too has doubts: Can't she follow more closely,
stay truer to the signals they've devised?
Their conversation shifts down into words,
then quickly upshifts, merges back

into the darkened lane where they can hear
droplets percussing onto roofs and windshields.
They grip the steering wheels. Once more their tires
spin puddles into mist.

III. *Every Creature's Version*

The Topiarist

for Abe

Out of a stately helical display
of shrubbery, new leaves poke into view:
The topiarist has been called away

or so I hope. Maybe his mind's astray,
letting once-hidden branches reach askew
out of a stately helical display.

Dignified structures spiked with disarray
regress to common unschooled English yew.
The topiarist has been called away

to shape his own life, and his protégé
has found its sense of humor. Look what grew
out of a stately helical display:

Stalks make alarming gestures as they sway
in wind, claiming the recognition due
the topiarist. He's been called away

and suddenly each leaf's on holiday.
A gentle spiral yields to curlicue
out of a stately helix: *Let us play!*
The topiarist has been called away.

Daphne's Regrets

I. (She sees a passerby)

You are not like him
    who stalked me here and staked me to my fright;
you were nowhere near
    when I became a coffin of my own.
I redden; winds have said that autumn does this,
    and that it's often autumn.
I soften all the pathways with my leaves,
    though no man will pursue me.
Soon I will be held in winter's sleep—
    they say it's often winter—
where I may see you in disordered dreams.
    The spring will kindly quench them.
Hail me when my dreams are turned to wood,
    a fresh brown ring of silence.

II. (The leaves console her)

On your branches we are ready now
      to dangle and to drop,
or instantly to crumble at the brush
      of couples passing by,
or even studiously turn to powder
      when someone's hand beholds us.
We are ready for some kind of leaving,
      no longer can be claimed.
Wear our gold tiara for the evening,
      our thirst and hunger bright!
Then lightening your boughs,
      spiralling to earth, we will salute you.
In spring your infant leaves will have
      no memory, no history of longing.

Garden Statues

We've faced another telling of the year,
        another trial by weather,
but never mind: the crocuses are here.
        We'll brace ourselves together,

afford the zealous honeybees' incursions,
        the afterthought of snow,
the refuse of cicadas and of pigeons,
        the floral overflow.

We'll hold the bare-veined leaves with their dismissal,
        their downward-shifting hue,
the stiffening of roots and boughs, the whistle
        of cold air speeding through,

the sleep invented by primordial reason,
        the dormancy of growing,
the chill of hearing every creature's version
        without one creature knowing.

The Voice of the Cicadas

Oh, sing! For we are seventeen today
and owe it to no victory but this:
The trees' tangled foundations where we lay
in darkness, mulling, crouched in insect bliss
below your feet, and guzzled timber sap—
these roots remained our bounty until now
and were not choked. We nestled in earth's lap
unmoved by your steam shovel or your plow,
and quite unmoved by reason or by "why,"
or by your face, though into it we've flown.
Five eyes to see, yet we have not one *I*;
Nourishing tuneful birds, we click and drone.
And all we crave to make our lives complete
is this monotonous history, to repeat.

Along the Potomac

I. The Cricket

If I were but a cricket at the ear
of this somnambulist whose mind, adrift,
allows his tideblown vessel to career
and spin, what wily quavers I would lift
into the vaporous region at his helm!
Forbidding sleep, I would uphold the dream
that launched his roving oars to scull this realm
where glancing waves stir up mute moonlight's gleam,
where babbling of jeweled fish belies
the depths of which they echo. I would guide
his hands to grasp the rudder, and his eyes
to seek Polaris, singing yet beside
his inner ear a song to school his heart,
encompassing his mind's unwavering art.

II. Cherry Blossom Time

Ricepaper-thin, pink petals dare the breeze
to catch them as they hurtle to the ground,
yet shudder if one breath is ill-at-ease
within their range of microscopic sound.
Clear observation falls as arrogance
upon them, your stark shadow gives them night,
they brave the wind but scatter at your glance.
You stare, and they embark in mimic flight.
Without a mien or purpose of their own
they lend each bough a temporary face,
till furrowless they dodge your shadow's frown
and flutter to some more idyllic place.
No motion rises in their hearts, nor will:
what wind alone created, it makes still.

The Snow Woman

Snow was the gentlest form of what I knew might happen.
Particles of ice, inwardly fused with slush,
contain my banishment. I guard the family door—
at least they had the heart to resurrect me here
instead of in the woods. Here I can see snowflakes
shuddering from coats when children hurry past me;
I can watch for signs—softening of brows,
lengthening of glances, even hands that may
eventually reach to pat my hardening shell.

IV. *Worth Restoring*

Midlife Interrogation

Are you now or have you ever been
      attractive?
Even as this fortune settles in,
you know its interest won't be retroactive.

Before Time pounces, he must go exploring:
With teasing lines he takes you for a spin,
      so seductive
you almost think your face is worth restoring.

So Sorry, Shall I Call Back Later?

But no, you only want me to *acknowledge*
that you stand dripping, dripping as we speak,
your phone's cord stretching, nipping at the towel edge—
you've *such* a way of flaunting your physique!

Call Waiting

You've struck gold in a telephonic mine:
Two sobbing women dangle from your line.
One wants to stay, the other will not go.
Just click that button twice: "Hello?"
                                          "Hello?"

Trading Up

It wasn't quite enough
rejoicing in each other
for qualities that overran the cup—

but, having checked the stars,
her broker, and his mother,
they're satisfied they both have traded up.

Pleasures Disproven

(Wherein the now-dispassionate
shepherd contemplates divorce)

O ecstasy,
O life of glee
if she'd agree
my Ex to be!

No broken necks,
no need to vex,
no sheepish sex—
just writing checks.

Upon Having Corrected an Accountant

A crustacean's demeanor is awful
when confronted for actions unlawful.
      Be prepared for a jab
      from the soft-centered crab,
though the battle may save you a clawful.

News of a Bull Market

A financial adviser to Pfizer
said, "This marketing couldn't be wiser:
      Whether curing his ills
      or enhancing his skills,
every man will pop pills as he plies her."

Colorization

On the revival of the miniskirt

At twenty-one her legs could stun.
At forty they're no duller.
The difference is, for the rerun
they're shown in Technicolor.

Disclaimer to Accompany "Love" Stamp

You think this stamp's romantic?
Offered "self-stick," I chose
to substitute semantic
for salivary woes.

Fame's Aftertaste

If you become a president or laureate or champ
you may expect to leave your mark upon a postage stamp:
Your face, however full or drawn, is daintily engraved
on perforated paper and in glassine packets saved;
your picture then becomes a seal of love, or debt, or news,
whose depth and innuendo we all know you did not choose.

But whether you're a publishing tycoon or gourmet cook
there are some implications that you'd best not overlook:
The sight of your small image may require a drink to follow,
for fame can have an aftertaste that's difficult to swallow;
and howsoever sterile be its words, you'll lend each missive
a less-than-sanitary state, unless you're self-adhesive.

Of course, this honor never comes before one's expiration
to ensure that honorees cannot dispute denomination—
no, neither can you name your price, nor choose the words within,
nor interview the other stamps with whom you may be seen.
But long before your face becomes an emblem to affix,
you'll have to have a noble soul, or at least a name that sticks.

Lactose Intolerance

Latinate nomenclature sure adds class:
I used to have to say, "Milk gives me gas."

Interdisciplinary Ode

(In honor of Dr. Gary D. Hack and Dr. Gwendolyn F. Dunn, two Maryland dentists who in 1995 discovered a hitherto unnoticed muscle.)

Congrats on the Sphenomandibularis!
May your success be longer than its name.
I know you weren't trying to embarrass
your colleagues in the sinus-drilling game,

nor those who scan the orbit of an eye,
or bear the globe upon a shoulder-socket,
or watch the wakefulness of nerves, or try
to pace the heart's exertions from a pocket.

You gladly would have shared your toothsome thoughts
with those anatomists whose grave denial
has robbed their books and handed off to poets
the task of telling why our eyes can smile.

Upon no other field have you impinged;
your jawboned colleagues needn't be unhinged.

Authority

Not only the teeth grow long:
In face of many snows,
your friends are calling "strong"
what once was a ski-slope nose.

A Falling-Out

(The tooth's swan song)

You've bitten off much more than I can chew, sir,
and our affiliation's getting looser.
We're going to have to call it quits, old friend.
Don't put it off—just one more bite—

THE END

Schadenfreud(e)

Poor Sigmund Freud, who in a tedious fashion
revealed that he could not account for passion,
pummeled bright scholars of the West to doubt
themselves and their perceptions—oh, what clout
he wielded!—casting in his wake a spell
of missing thoughts and objects. Private hell
for all dreamers to share, this fit him neatly:
his name translates to "joy," but incompletely.

Song of the Off-Duty Psychiatrist

I'm feeling "inappropriate" today —
lame euphemism, but at least it limps
where logic creeps. Don't look at me that way.

I gave all at the office. I'm *blasé*.
Who wouldn't be? What a parade of gimps!
I'm feeling inappropriate. Today

They crowded me, telling me what to say,
pursuing me—wild satyrs, wicked nymphs,
illogical creeps! Don't look at me that way —

I'll name *your* passions till they melt away,
then medicate you like those other wimps —
I'm feeling inappropriate today!

All right, all right, you've had a good display
of how this work distorts me. Yes, it crimps
my logic. Cripes, don't look at me that way!

It's just that, when I thought all disarray
was cured by naming it, there came a glimpse
of feeling. Inappropriate today;
logic *must* creep..... Don't *look* at me that way!

Millennium WWWitches' Brew

Our "www"
has toiled hard to trouble you
to snore your life away
since before the Y2K.

By the clicking of your digits,
something animated fidgets
into pictures sharp or runny
that will drain your time and money.

Open links! Whoever blinks
in our Lethean cauldron sinks.

Preparing for a Visit

I know you're not too fond of books, Mother, so I've arranged
a subtly tinted goblet on each shelf. You'll think I've changed
and kiss my aging forehead tenderly, turning to note
the scent of household cleaners. *Then* you'll remove your coat.
Is that your car I hear now? It's time to put aside
reflection, grab the doorknob, swallow hard, and open wide.

Vitreous Floater

Are you a diving partner of the mote
that swam into one eye and never vanished?
Eerily focused, you have learned to float
inside my field of vision, undiminished.
You must have photographs of me someplace—
no, none that would embarrass or surprise
unless with dewy ignorance of face
and camera-ready, all-or-nothing eyes.
How quickly did they darken in your tray?
They haunted you, or you would not be here
hunting for them each time I look away,
loitering in the margins when I'm near,
never content to have instilled your story
into this vessel of *mementi mori.*

V. *Audit*

Angel Encounter

The visitor who joined with me
one day when days were commonplace,
who taught my childish eyes to see
the candlelight that formed his face—
how disappointed I will be
if he was just some traveler from space
and not eternity.

Encounter II

Removing from the grocer's siren shelf
a flimsy box bulging with ginger Santas,
I turn a corner, hear a flurry, stop
somewhere between the herring and the greetings.

But why has he waited for this evening,
this aisle, to let me know that he still hovers?
And all the while his wings beat the cold air
into a silent, sugarless meringue.

Findings

Follow the guides
you have written as whims,
inventions and findings —

Follow them backward and find
what traces behind them
into them:

You are a comet sailing through
this body and mind
keeping them in order,

You are the kernel wobbling in a shell,
the apple rocking in a wooden bowl,
the pen in a wavering hand,

touching
one point
at a time.

The Perfect Word

You guard one perfect word there in your chest;
there it nestles, advising you to listen.
With thump, and thump, and clench, that shiny fist
apportions blood, embraces, and demands:
        "Now think! Think! Think!" it musters you
in tones that only you can hear,
        "You must! You must! You must!"

It makes you sing, insists you find its mate,
echoes when you speak the truth,
freezes when you lie,
shudders when you compromise.

No breath, no wish avoids its careful scrutiny
or rides without its skipping beat—
        "Apace, apace, apprentice!"
Apprenticed you are, for all your days and nights:
obeyed or disobeyed
it will master you.

To the Evening Sky

Nature's bequest gives nothing but doth lend,
And, being frank, she lends to those are free.
—William Shakespeare, Sonnet IV

What's in these hands pretends to be my own,
including every unexamined hour
that falls between them, spent before it's known.
What lens might I obtain to square the power
of days divided up by small demands?
And yet how indivisible that space
of several seconds, in whose chamber stands
a scope to look upon your wise old face!
Your magnitude I won't pretend to fill
with sage remarks; no longer do I fear
your darkness might consume me—though it will.
Against that day you'll swiftly commandeer,
let it be learned by what spark I am driven:
these hands are empty, save what they have given.

A Fault

You may have wondered if I'd toppled off
the earth—or rather, since each earthly ledge
points inward, tumbled over one to wedge
myself in some oozing infernal trough.
A fitting end, you think? Well, fair enough:
My rate of correspondence teased the edge
of zero, tried your patience. No, don't hedge
the question. Now that earth gives a good cough
and heaves me to its gentle crust, to grovel
before my would-be rescuers (who scowl,
forgivably, to see my face again),
I realize why so few had grabbed a shovel:
Silence seems arrogant. Better to howl
and chatter than to use, and lose, the pen.

Lost Satellite

Where is the roundness that created you,
explorer, hunter, scavenger, lost child?
Even now as you wander from your sphere,
how readily you twirl about another.

Where is the roundness that created you?

The shaved ribbon reclaims it as a curl,
the cratered face endures it as a shadow,
the bitten moon refills itself in creatures
who scan the night for one another's eyes.

Ripples in the Fabric

"April 3,1992: George Smoot of Lawrence Berkeley Laboratory announces discovery of 'ripples in the fabric of space-time' that created galaxies and empty space."
—Washington Post, *May 3,1992*

Of ripples in the fabric of space-time
we are alerted: in a place once blank
they spring from meter and inherit rhyme.

How like the growing nautilus's climb
is our galactic spiral, as a bank
of ripples in the fabric of space-time

where human words may radiate sublime
reflections, reasoned acts: what careless prank
could spring from meter and inherit rhyme?

Must we, like some inchoate mollusk, slime
back into an abandoned shell that sank
from ripples in the fabric of space-time?

Or else, emerging from that paradigm,
can we escape this sluggish holding-tank
and ripple through the fabric of space-time,
springing from meter, inheriting rhyme?

To One Who Listens

(After touring NASA's model of Space Station "Freedom")

I speak to one who listens
with ear held to the ground,
who hears encrusted branches snap
and steps resound;

who lends the rains and breezes
that cool a silent face;
who mixes, leavens, chills, and bakes
the bread of space.

I speak to one who glistens
behind a starry tent,
enticing us with clues to scale
the firmament.

Our words—are they but markers
for where our breath has gone,
Ozymandian apologies
for skies not won?

Audit

We regret to tell you
your grief is nondeductible.
How can you say we've overlooked
anything of value?

Yours is a flimsy claim
considering you never had
declared what you now say you've lost,
nor given it a name.

Its image is not here:
no videos, no sonograms,
no proofs, no matte or glossy stills,
no negatives appear.

It is not itemized
with duplicate receipts,
appraisals, or certificates
like something truly prized.

No doctor or garage bills,
no dents or missing eyeteeth—
and yet our file on you has grown
like clumps of random cells.

When next we reconvene
Let's hope for resolution.
Substantiate your sorrow: Bring
things we can say we've seen.

The Old Year

New is the year; let's bury the old.
Carting it out to the woods, I hold
my nose from this beast that's refused to just leave.
My brain, heart, and stomach continue to heave.

New is the year; let's shut off the old,
a useless appliance encrusted with mold.
But what was it built for? Shall I believe
It's *meant* to unravel what fibers we weave?

New is the year; let's silence the old
and trash the libretto before it's retold.
Outliving regret, let's sing more than grieve
for arias buried in recitative.

Biographical Note

Claudia Gary-Annis is a poet, composer, editor, and freelance writer who lives in the Washington, D.C. area. Her poems have appeared in *The Formalist, Edge City Review, Light, The Lyric, Pivot, Sparrow, Medicinal Purposes, Neovictorian/Cochlea, Orbis (U.K.)*, and other literary journals, as well as a number of newspapers and newsletters, Web journals, and anthologies. Her chapbook *Ripples in the Fabric* was published in 1996 by Somers Rocks Press, and her more recent chapbook, *Schadenfreud(e) and Other Occupational Hazards,* was published in 2004 by Musings Press. She has given readings in many east coast cities and has taught poetry workshops for adults and children. Former poetry editor of *Edge City Review* and founding editor-publisher of *Musings from Northern Virginia,* she is currently northern regional vice president of the Poetry Society of Virginia and senior editor of *Vietnam* Magazine.

Her musical works, which have been performed in a number of U.S. cities, include chamber music and art songs based on poems by Shakespeare, Marvell, and Heine as well as contemporary poets including Dana Gioia, Frederick Turner, Phillis Levin, Frederick Feirstein, Marilyn Marsh Noll, and others. One of her songs—a setting for soprano, violin, and cello of Shakespeare's Sonnet XVIII ("Shall I compare thee to a summer's day?")—appeared in issue 60 of *Sparrow, the Yearbook of the Sonnet.* For more information see her Web site (http://claudiagary.home.att.net).

Artist's Statement

The medallion on the cover, "Juliet," is the work of sculptor Daniel Riccio. Inspired by a dialog between the artist and the author, "Juliet" was formed in wax and cast in bronze using the ancient art of lost-wax casting. Riccio works in forms both classical and innovative at his Connecticut studio, and teaches metalsmithing at Central Connecticut State University. More of his creations can be glimpsed at http://www.danielriccio.com.

Printed in the United States
128692LV00012BA/136/A